MY FIRST
Gymnastics
Class

By Alyssa Satin Capucilli
Photographs by Laura Hanifin

Ready-to-Read

Simon Spotlight
New York   London   Toronto   Sydney   New Delhi

This book was previously published with slightly different text and art.

For Molly Isabelle, our newest tumbler!

—A.S.C.

SIMON SPOTLIGHT
An imprint of Simon & Schuster Children's Publishing Division
1230 Avenue of the Americas, New York, New York 10020
This Simon Spotlight edition June 2016
Text copyright © 2012 by Alyssa Satin Capucilli
Photographs and illustrations copyright © 2012 by Simon & Schuster, Inc.
For information about special discounts for bulk purchases, please contact Simon & Schuster Special Sales at
1-866-506-1949 or business@simonandschuster.com.
Manufactured in the United States of America 0816 LAK
2   4   6   8   10   9   7   5   3
Library of Congress Cataloging-in-Publication Data
Names: Capucilli, Alyssa Satin, 1957–
Title: My first gymnastics class / by Alyssa Satin Capucilli ; photographs by Laura Hanifin.
Description: This Simon Spotlight hardcover/paperback edition. | New York : Simon Spotlight, [2016] |
©2012. | Series: Ready-to-Read | Audience: Ages: 3–5.
Identifiers: LCCN 2016003218 | ISBN 9781481461870 (paperback : alk. paper) |
ISBN 9781481461894 (hardcover : alk. paper) | ISBN 9781481461900 (eBook)
Subjects: LCSH: Gymnastics for children—Juvenile literature.
Classification: LCC GV464.5 .C33 2016 | DDC 796.44083—dc23
LC record available at http://lccn.loc.gov/2016003218
This book was previously published with slightly different text and art.

It is my very first
gymnastics class!

This leotard is

just right for me.

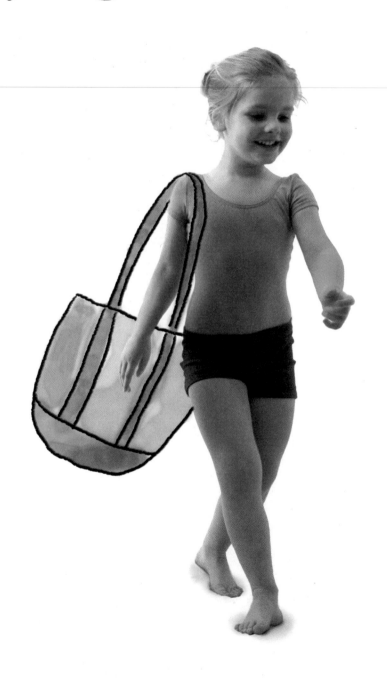

Now that I am ready to go,

I wonder what I will see.

We stand on the mat,
straight and tall.

Then we jump and
stretch our arms wide.

We warm up our bodies
as we touch our toes.

We bend and reach
to each side!

We learn a pike.

We learn a tuck.

We learn a straddle, too.

"It takes practice,"
Coach Rose says.

There are so many things we can do!

We can leap like frogs.

We can spin like logs.

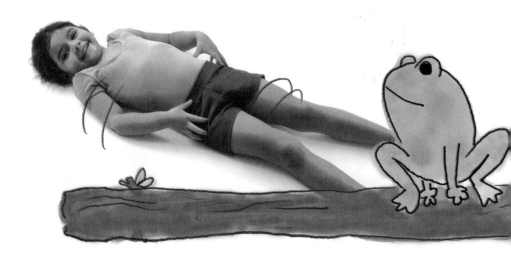

We can hop just like
kangaroos!

We can walk like a
tightrope walker.

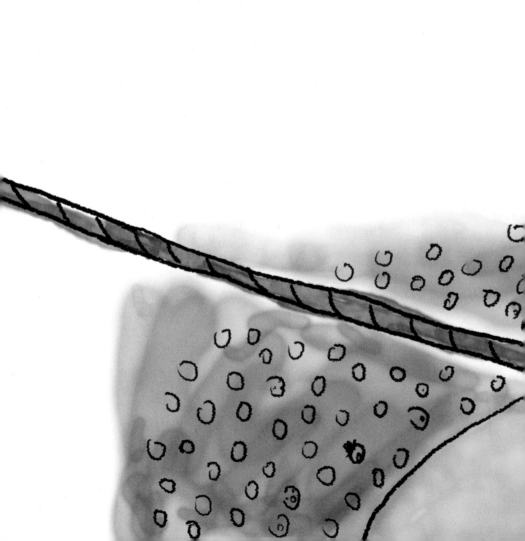

We balance just like they do!

Hands up high.

Head down low.

I can roll like a ball.

Off I go!

Soon I will be ready to jump, swing, and climb!

Gymnastics is fun!
I had a great time!

Do you want to be a gymnast?

Don't forget to find a grown-up to

help you read and learn about the

gymnastics moves in this book!

Warm up!

1 Stand Tall

Stand straight and tall on your mat or a soft surface. Keep your feet together and arms at your side. You look like the letter I!

Now jump! Open your legs and arms wide. Now you look like a big letter X!

2 Jump and Stretch

Jump again and close your arms and legs.

Jump wide and clap your hands over your head. Get your muscles nice and warm.

3
Touch Your Toes

Start with your legs wide. See the triangle between your legs?

Can you touch your toes?

First try to touch one foot and then the other.
No tickling now!

4
Walk Like a Spider

Pretend you are a spider! Put your hands on the floor and walk around. Be careful not to bump into any other spiders!

Pike, Tuck, and Straddle

1 Pike

Sit up straight and tall with your
legs out in front of you.

No bent knees! That's a pike!

2 Tuck

Now bring your feet in as close to your body as you can.

Give your knees a big hug.

That's a super tuck!

3 Straddle

Open sesame!

Can you stretch your legs as wide as a rainbow?

Now flop over like a rag doll.

That's a great straddle stretch!

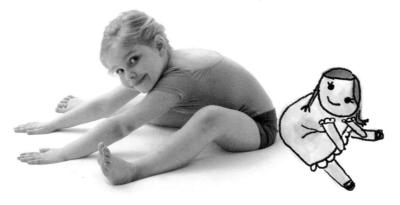

Leap, Roll, Hop, Balance

1 Leap

Start standing tall.

Bend both knees . . .

then jump.

Try a small jump.

Then try a bigger jump too.

Ribbit! Ribbit!

How far can your frog go?

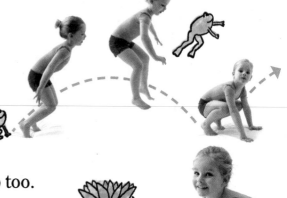

2 Roll

Can you lie on your back like a long log?

Here comes a big wind! Roll and spin, roll and spin.

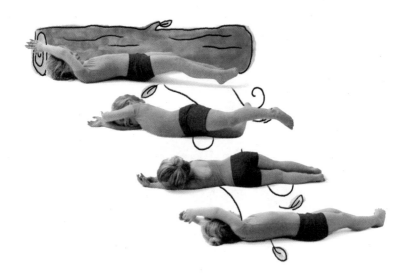

3 Hop

Hop, hop, hop.
Try to make small hops on two legs.
Then hop, hop, hop on one leg.
Boing!
Keep your knees nice and soft
just like a kangaroo does.

4 Balance

Gymnasts learn to balance on a thin beam of wood.
Let's practice on a piece of colorful tape first.
Can you put one foot in front of the
other without stepping off the tape?
Keep your arms out to your sides
to help. Good job!

Roll like a ball

Don't forget to ask a grown-up
to help you try this move!

1

Stand straight and tall like a candle.

Put both hands on the mat. Now curl up as round as a ball.

2

Keep your chin tucked into your chest.

That way, the top of your head won't touch the floor.

Gently rock forward and roll over.

Keep your eyes on your belly!

A grown-up can help you do it just right.

Ta-da!

You did it!

Soon you'll be jumping on the trampoline and swinging on the bars.

Gymnastics is fun!